Overcoming Life's Challenges

Ricardo McCalpin

Order this book online at www.trafford.com/09-0556
or email orders@trafford.com

Most Trafford titles are also available at major online book retailers.

Note for Librarians: A cataloguing record for this book is available from Library
and Archives Canada at www.collectionscanada.ca/amicus/index-e.html

Printed in Victoria, BC, Canada.

ISBN: 978-1-4269-1115-6 (sc)

*We at Trafford believe that it is the responsibility of us all, as both individuals and corporations, to make choices
that are environmentally and socially sound. You, in turn, are supporting this responsible conduct each time you
purchase a Trafford book, or make use of our publishing services. To find out how you are helping, please visit
www.trafford.com/responsiblepublishing.html*

*Our mission is to efficiently provide the world's finest, most comprehensive book publishing service, enabling
every author to experience success. To find out how to publish your book, your way, and have it available
worldwide, visit us online at www.trafford.com/10510*

 www.trafford.com

North America & international
toll-free: 1 888 232 4444 (USA & Canada)
phone: 250 383 6864 ♦ fax: 250 383 6804 ♦ email: info@trafford.com

The United Kingdom & Europe
phone: +44 (0)1865 487 395 ♦ local rate: 0845 230 9601
facsimile: +44 (0)1865 481 507 ♦ email: info.uk@trafford.com

10 9 8 7 6 5 4 3 2 1

CONTENT

Acknowledgement   1

Introduction   2-3

Introduction to my life in August Town   4-37

Spiritual Realms

Understanding Life   38-40

Acquisition of Knowledge   41-43

Acknowledge the Almighty   44-49

Establish a Purpose   50-52

The Almighty's Will Versus Human Desires   53-56

Communicate with the Almighty   57-62

Spirituality Versus Religion   63-66

Seek Moral Piety   67-68

Academic-Professional Development

Looking through the mind's eyes   69-71

Developing a strong character in the mind   72-74

Hope Versus Faith   75-76

Perseverance   77-79

Dedication Versus Making Commitment   80-81

Decision Making   82-83

Get involved in physical activities   84-88

Strength Versus Weakness   89-91

Winning Versus Losing   92-93

Love Versus Hatred   94-95

Humility Versus Aggression   96-98

Surpassing Mistakes   99-101

Personal Development

Personal Development   102-106

Evaluate your Life   107-114

Acknowledgement

I would like to thank the Almighty for instilling in me his inspiration and wisdom to write this book. I am also grateful to my parents and brothers who have given me full support in my writing career. I would also like to thank my mentor for giving me the motivation throughout the years by helping to develop my professionalism. I want to extend gross respect to my friends Gregory Waite and Garth Whyte for all the important conversations we had that lead to all the great insights which is used in this book.

I want to thank all the people who help to type the scripts and Raymond Ulett for providing the computer which help in the final production of the document. I want to thank Yanique Hall, Pauline McKenzie and Sheree O'Sullivan for helping to proofread the entire book. Last but not least, I extend gratitude to Ricardo Simpson for being supportive in allowing me to browse his internet and printing certain articles.

Introduction

Overcoming Life's Challenges-is a challenge for every human being as we all faces temptations which can prevent us from making it to paradise and obstacles which can cause academic and personal failures in our lives. It is a very inspirational book; because it outlines many of the problems that we have or will encounter throughout our lives.

It gives clear and concise information on how we can overcome these obstacles. It is important to overcome them; because they are the determining factors for our failures or success in life. The reason for writing this book is to basically give people a guideline in approaching life. Therefore I chose to address issues which will permit us to reach the paradigm of our horizon.

Once human beings are able to master these 3 aspects of life they stand a better chance to, Overcome Life's Challenges; (1) Spiritual realms, (2) Academic-professional development and (3) Personal development.

It is unique in its own rights as it gives a step by step approach to life in 22 topics; by which individuals can follow in order to **"overcome life's**

challenges." The writing styles are diverse in order to facilitate the different learning styles of human beings. It gives problems & solutions, comparison & contrast, cause & effect, rhetorical questions, definitions and theories and also practical examples to foster clear understanding. Agglomerations of teenagers are lost during a period of their life and this book could erase that possibility once read by them.

In this book I have shared a number of thoughts (secrets) which I am sure are important in facilitating individuals to achieve success in life. I really believe that thoughts are golden and they should be shared in order to enlighten others on the unthinkable knowledge and inspirations, which can prevent many of our brothers and sisters down fall in life.

OVERCOMING LIFE'S CHALLENGES

I spent all my life in a small community called Hermitage of Greater

August Town located in Eastern St. Andrew. August Town was formerly called

African Hill; however the name was change after the slaves were emancipated

on August 1, 1838. The month of August represented a sense of freedom to

the slaves from the Mona Estate who acquired lands in August Town after they

received full freedom at the end of the apprenticeship system. Our

communities lie between two hills on the eastern and western parts of the

community. The Hope River with its source high in the water catchment area

of the Blue Mountain peak runs through parts of the communities and forms

its mouth in the Bull Bay Sea. This river was used by the Great Alexander

Bedward as a healing stream. "He said the river contained healing properties

and it subsequently became the healing stream." H.E.S Woods (Shakepeare)

started the movement; which Bedward inherited in Dallas Castle and later

moved to August Town. Alexander Bedward was ordained by Woods as a

prophet amongst his congregation; thus he leaved the community and went

back to Spanish Town. Bedward lead the congregation between 1891 and

1921, and formed a mass movement called "Bedwardism" comprised of his ministers and deacons, and followers from across the island.

Many people from all over the country usually walk miles to come and worship with the preacher in their quest to be healed. He built and monumental church where his worship took place. This structure was located above his healing stream where the baptism of his followers took place. His popularity earned for him the title of a folk hero in Jamaica. He is deemed a prophet by many people from across the Caribbean; specifically Panama and Cuba, thus his teachings lives on in the heart of many people. His followers continued to gather and worship at his home which was named Union Camp. He was arrested in 1921 after leading a march into the city of Kingston and placed in an Asylum; where he died several years later. However there are only two remaining Bedwardites living today.

Our community is an historic place as one of Jamaica's living legend in Reggae music; Sizzla Kalonji also resides in the plains of Bedward Gardens, the same river that Bedward and his followers once utilized. Sizzla Kalonji seems to benefit from some of the spiritual gifts which have been bestowed in this valley. The Hope River ending in August Town is clustered as the hills joins at the mouth of the river making it difficult for the water to leave the community; likewise it is difficult for individuals to successfully rise from the community.

As you go along Hermitage Road and the further down you go, the potholes becomes wider and the more your opportunities begin to diminish. Mona Road represents the highway of success for many persons across the country and the world. As within walking distances are two of the largest universities in the Caribbean; the University of the West Indies which began in 1948 and the University of Technology. However, despite all these positives, the negative influences seems to be a powerful force that rapidly propels many of our youths in the doldrums of prisons.

In my childhood days, many of us dreamt of attending one of the Universities in order to make our families proud. As we grew older a lot of us found it more difficult to elevate from the community as our faith was clustered by a political division and a lack of opportunity. The political division and the lack of opportunity represent the two hills that border the community. Life in August Town was not conducive to self development; as the living condition was below poverty line in some areas. Regardless of all these experiences, I had to examine the pros and cons of both the positive and negative experiences and make a decision to be successful in life.

Living in August Town, people are exposed to a lot of obstacles such as, the availability of illegal weapons, exposure to crime and violence, unemployment and lack of education. I was exposed to some of these obstacles also, but I was able to overcome them because I do not blame situations but seek ways to combat them. One could also look around in their community for the good example set by persons who grew in the same situation as themselves. Therefore I can identify some very influential persons from my community such as Dr. Peter Phillips, Prof. Barry Chevannes, Patrick Ewing, Etana and Nicole Grant. However I will highlight the struggle of Nicole Grant who overcame her obstacles in life and became successful. Though many people's main dream is to own a home came very late in their lives, Nicole Grant at the age of 28 owned her first home and at age 33 has achieved 3 beautiful houses. She is a very outstanding National Hockey player who plays for Jamaica and is one of the country's top Goal scorers for the past 16 years and is currently the National Hockey Team Captain. She was also chosen as one of the

Tournament's MVP in the 2007 Caribbean Hockey Championship held in Trinidad, where Jamaica was the silver medalist. Nicole is a member of Tropics Hockey Club where she hold the position of Club and team captain who has lead her team to many victories over the years, including 2007 Premier League Title and 2008 Six-A-Side and Indoor Tournaments for the Jamaica Hockey Federation.

Nicole is the proud mother of her 4 years old son Atario Brown, who presently attends St. Peter & Paul Preparatory School. He attended Junior World & Activity Centre for the first 3 and half years of his life. Though no longer a student at that school Nicole Grant was admired for her hard work and involvement in the school, by the owner and principal thus she was made a member of the school board.

She is a very compassionate and unselfish young lady. Though one of her main life goal has already been achieved she did so while helping others, especially members of her own family and close friends. Her achievement came through share determination and a drive to change her life from poverty and to emancipate herself from the ills of her community which was riddled with violence.

Nicole was born to a family of 15, 2 girls and 13 boys. She was the 10th child for her father who had 13 and the last or "washbelly" of her mother who had 7, 2 girls and 5 boys. She was born and raised with her mother and 7 siblings in the community of August Town, in the Hermitage area. Her mother Eileen Rattray, who is a very strong and well admired woman in the community, was forced to be the sole bread winner of the family when her father migrated to the United States at the age of 5.

With so many children to feed, rent to pay and utility bills her mother found it very difficult as she was not getting any help from the children's father. Often times there were little or no food in the house, therefore many nights she went to bed hungry. Her mother found it difficult to pay the bills and for many years she lived without electricity in the house and running water in the pipe.

She attended August Town Primary School and during her primary school years, there was a period when she had no shoes to wear but that did not deter her from going to school. She went bare feet everyday; though she had to walk approximately 1.5 miles to school. Going to school without lunch money was the norm for her. She was a very happy and active child who laughs at almost everything, there was no way you could tell she was having problems at home. She was not successful in her Common Entrance which surprised her teachers because she was a very brilliant child who has always performed as one of the top students in the class. When asked by her teacher what contributed to her mal-performance in the examination, she told the teacher that she never wanted to pass her common entrance as her mother could not afford to send her to a high school. At that time there was a compulsory fee to attend High School.

She moved on to Mona Secondary School in 1987 which was also walking distant from her home. Mona Secondary however was upgraded the following year to a High School. Though already a lover of school she was more determined to get a solid education when at age 12. However on her first day attending high school she came home to find all her mother's furniture on the side of the street. The landlord had evicted her mother due to non- payment of rent. She was rescued by her God Mother who also lived in the community. She could barely manage as she too had 7 children to whom sole responsibility was granted. Soon I was sent back to live with her mother who was now living in a one room apartment with all the children.

To alleviate herself from the stresses of her situation Nicole became a very active member of her Club and school's netball teams since the age of 10. She was such a good netballer that she was sent on trial for the national team. However she was not successful as she was told that her height was a factor. She was just too short by the Jamaica Netball Association standard. However, that did not affect her ability to play as she continued to play for her school and Club.

During her High School years she was introduced to hockey at age 15 and her first encounter was with Tropics Hockey Club even before she played school girl hockey. She became a national Hockey representative at age 16; at the under 19 level. There she continued to play Hockey for her club and country.

Her secret was to stay at school for the entire day so that she did not have to go home to the barking of guns which was prevalent in the community. Therefore she would leave home at 7am and return home at 7pm. Her typical day was attending school, extra classes and then across the road to the hockey field for club or national training that usually begins at 5pm to 7pm.

She enjoyed playing Hockey and was also inspired by the members of the Hockey fraternity at the time. They would take her to their homes and exposed her to things she never thought was possible, such as driving in a motor car, having access to open a refrigerator, watching colour television, taking a warm water shower and having a proper meal.

This kind of exposure motivated her to do well because all the people she was exposed to at the Hockey Federation were career oriented. She then saw firsthand that having a good career through education can make your life better.

At Mona she was very successful at all her CXC exams though she had to study by her gate in order to get light from the street, as there was no electricity in her house at the time. She then moved on to St. Hugh's High School 6th form to pursue her Advanced Level Exams. During her first years at St. Hugh's High school she revived hockey which was dormant for many years. She was awarded the school's highest award in sports for the two years she was a student at the institution. She was also overall champion girl in track and field.

During her high school years she would do odd jobs of washing people's clothes and household cleaning to make her lunch money for school. Her mother was always there for her and would give her whatever she could afford.

While at St. Hugh's the violence in the community had gotten worst and getting home at nights after her daily activities at school and training with her club as well as the National Hockey teams proved more and more dangerous. She then asked a friend who was a member of her club and the president of the Hockey Federation at that time to take her in until she had completed her Advanced Level Exams and she was facilitated.

Nicole was successful at her advanced level exams and went to the University of the West Indies (Mona), immediately after leaving St. Hugh's High School. During University Nicole had to leave her friend's home and went back to live in Hermitage to take care of her 2 five year old nieces, as her mother and sister had migrated to the United States. It took a while for them to get settled in the USA and so the burden was left on her to take care of the kids financially. She would use her lunch money as well as other from summer jobs to pay the bills and take care of the kids.

During her final year at the University; her closest brother who sometimes helped out got killed by the police in Westmoreland. This was another police senseless killing that is very prevalent in Jamaica. She was then faced with the burden of planning and partially financing the funeral as her mother and sister were unable to come to Jamaica at that time.

This really had a serious effect on her as she was greatly affected by the loss. She however found her strength in close friends and the Almighty God as she is a practicing Catholic. She then had to take on helping to finance the education of his two little daughters who he left behind. Approximately one year later her favorite male cousin who was with her at the time, was brutally murdered by gun men in the community. This was another death that totally depressed her. Then the following year her nephew led gangs from nearby areas, into the community where 4 men were shot and injured. Her depression got worse especially where almost every night there was gun fire and someone got killed who was either a friend or someone she knew. Her depression also came about also by the feeling of entrapment. She felt trapped in the community.

After leaving University it took her about 7 months to get a job. She worked, took care of the home and kids until her sister was able to take her child. She was able to also save and from her savings deposited on a home the first chance she got.

She is now a very successful business woman who owns her own business in the field of Computer Software and IT sales and service. She always said that it doesn't matter where or what your circumstances are, you will become what you want to be. She believes that it is imperative that you look at your strength and build on it rather than worry over your weakness. She also believes that adversities in life are very important to experience; because it makes you stronger and more compassionate towards others as you too remember how it felt when you were in that situation. Her story is very inspirational and motivational as she reflected tremendous strength as a woman. My upbringing was alike her in many ways and we both are hoping to continue making positive contributions to humanity.

Many of our young men became prey to gang leaders who use them to fulfill their political agenda. These young men were trained to hate other citizens from different parts of the communities. Their influence was internal because they were not exposed to any other life outside the community. A lot of them do not have an understanding of why they are fighting the wars. It is important for teenagers to be exposed to people from different levels of society, so they can get various perspectives on life. My mentor, Mr. Trevor Morgan played an important role in developing my professionalism as a young man. This has given me a different outlook on life which influences me to strive for success. Being exposed to different types of people that I have met while playing football all across the island and attending college, I garnered an understanding of the causes of many of our failures and also how to overcome life's challenges.

The large potholes in the community, are symbolic to the shambolic state of the community as zinc fences forms a juxtapose along the road ways of Bryce Hill, Duppy Lane, Jungle Twelve and African Gardens. Many people blame these situations for their inability to succeed but some of us were made stronger as it instilled in us the drive to become successful. While many people allow negative situations to overcome them, I combat them by studying more often, training harder, writing songs, poems and books. Thus I am urging everyone to do something productive during their spare time which can improve our situation in the future. Politics plays a very powerful role in shaping our society; thus it forms a division in our community which has stifled the potential of an abundance of our people. Our community is multicultural and multidenominational; with our African descendants outnumbering those of Indian descent. Inculcated in our community are different denominations such as Jehovah Witnesses, Church of God, Sabbath Churches and Revivalism. However it is the people of African descents who are killing each others. It is time for Black people to awake themselves and realize that we are responsible for holding down our race. We need to acknowledge our powers and unite in our effort in, **"Overcoming Life's Challenges."** No race is superior to us but we need to support and build our people by building Africa. I want to share a quotation from Dee Lee, a financial educator; I quote, **"They are still our slaves, we continue to reap profits from Blacks without the effort of physical slavery. Look at the methods of containment that they use on themselves: ignorance, greed and selfishness."** It is time our people refrain from pushing our personal initiative and support an effort which will tackle our central problems. This must be done collaboratively; as it cannot be done by any single individual. I do agree that most of our Black organizations are very purposeful; but for us to be more effective it is to join effort. It does not make any sense to use our money to hold meetings at their luxurious hotels and not accomplishing the task of uplifting our people. I think those budgets used to hold meetings could be used to develop businesses or programmes which can affect positive changes in the lives of the less fortunate. A lot of people get involved in revivalism and lodge to gain riches at our own people distraught. Thus they sell their souls to manipulate the spirit world in their quest to keep others down. I am not spreading a message of hatred against any set of people; but I am imploring that we should help our people from their sufferation.

Another challenge, we all faces is deterioration in moral values in our society due to a rapid change cause by modernization and globalization. This wipes away our traditionalistic society; which was built on Godly principles, moral values and discipline. Thus, I grew in a time when many men were ignorant to the blessing of having a virtuous woman and women being ignorant to identifying the qualities of a real man. Therefore, we were exposed to bad examples of relationships which proved to be detrimental to our spiritual, professional-academical and personal development. Women are very important in human development; thus men should seek virtuosity in them. Recently, I have been reflecting on their purpose and realized they are the axis on which the world changes. They influence the behaviours of men, for instance in certain secondary schools in Jamaica; the girls started to admire boys who bleach their faces and that became a trend. Others yield to pressure in order to fit in to the pattern. In other schools where the girl's value intelligent boys it created a channel for good performance from the boys; even the not so brilliant have to upgrade their selves; in order to fit into their social groups. Women are very powerful; therefore I am urging them to strive for biblical principles because they worth more than materialistic values. It was made clear in Proverbs 31:10 and I quote, "A capable, intelligent, and virtuous woman-who is he who can find her? She is far more precious than jewels and her value is above rubies or pearls." Hence, whenever a man found her; he should keep and care her. In verse 12, it is stated that, "She comforts, encourages, and does him only good as long as there is life within her." Hence women should play a positive and supportive role in their men's lives and offer comfort as needed. She should also help him become the best person he can possible be. She should strive for virtuosity; as it is the best recognition women can acquire. In verse 28, it is declared, "Her children rise up and called her blessed and her husband boast of and praises her." It was further emphasized in verse 29, "Many daughters have done virtuously, nobly and well, but you excel them all." Women should also seek spirituality over physical beauty and this was emphasized in verse 30, "Charm and grace are deceptive, and beauty is vain, but who reverently and worshipfully fears the lord, she shall be praised." In the ancient world many wars between great nations such as the

Trojans and the Spartans were started by power struggle, greed or women. I am sure many of you have seen the movie, "TROY"; and you would have realized that the war which ended the life of the prince of the Trojan's Army, was started over a woman. We also faced a similar case in August Town; as blood were shed, house bombed, families disintegrated and lives lost. People need to begin to read their holy books; as these biblical happenings and prophecies are happening inside every highways and byways of the globe. I personally study those words laid out by the Almighty and try to live by them; in my quest of **"Overcoming life's Challenges."**

My desire to help my family forces me to strive for excellence. Honestly my family is very important because they are the people who had faith in me when others doubted my ability. A lot of people in my community regarded us as the worst set of human beings; thus it prompted me to remain focus on, **"Overcoming life's challenges."** It is the hardest thing for children to grow in a community where there is a lack of respect for their family. My cousins and I were treated with prejudice and bias in our quest to represent our football team; even though our talents were superior to other youths we were not selected. This influences me to spread a message to the world that the Almighty is real and living today. I am positive about this; as he is the one who strategies and structure my life through desolate situations. The creator speaks in us and I can testify about that. It happened in many situations in my sleep and also when I am awake. For instance, I wanted to write a script to submit to the principal as a part of the college pledge competition. However, the inspiration came one night when I was sleeping in my room at college. I awoke with the words in my head and quickly written them in my book. I then wake my friends and told them that I have the college pledge and I read it to them. My friend Paul Bogle then adds his part to it; my other friends started reciting it and made a statement that this is the winning script.

The turning point of my life came when I met an angel (my mentor) sent by the Almighty, who have help me to make the decision to attend college.

I went to G.C. foster college where I trained to become a teacher. It helped me to become more independent and professional. Thus I was able to acquire a diploma in education and a Bachelor of physical education. It was at G.C Foster my writing career began to develop; hence I have received a great accomplishment of co- writing the college pledge along with my friend Paul

Bogle. I am sure everyone would like to see the pledge; therefore I will make it available.

I stand as the beam of light

I promise to act against indignation

And look towards the future with tolerance and sight

Through academics and sports I will be the greatest in my fight

In the darkest place I am sure my light will always shine

I promise to help behold your excellence;

And to molds Jamaica's children to become productive members of society

I promise to remain flexible in a changing society

With pride and dignity

I will always stand for equality

Failing never to hold high my school motto

A sound mind, in a sound body

Therefore I am imploring all individuals to gain an education. This is the most powerful tool which can transform an individual's life and allows us to transcend social, political and geographical boundaries. Too many of our people feel as if a high school education should be their limit, but we should all try to obtain the highest level in this competitive world. "Youths, give yourselves a chance to live comfortable in this world." We should also seek to develop our talents by keeping focus on the things which are important to our longevity. Too much of our time are being wasted doing activities for pleasure, we need to develop a culture which fosters productivity. Hence instead of spending a lot of time partying, use that time and probably write a book, movie, practice to cook, sew etc. I suggest that individuals set timetables and follow the set procedures in order to effectively manage their time throughout each day.

We need to do productive things from we are young. A lot of us have it the wrong way, as we believe in having fun while we are young and work hard when we get old. This traditionalistic view that we are too young to lead is practice by people in governance and in society on a whole. This view has help in crippling the innovations of the young energetic and brilliant individuals; who are graduating from college; likewise it affect youth development in our community.

There are biblical and empirical evidences which proves that this traditionalistic view is incorrect and need to change. Somewhere in the bible it was stated that the children will lead the way and also there are real life

scenarios, but I will mention a story about Tiffany Richards a twelve year old

girl who graduated from the North Carolina University with a Bachelors Degree

in 2006. She is now working as a secretary in the White House in Washington

D.C. I believe we should take advice and directions from the elders but we also

need the opportunity to implement our innovative strategies and

development in technology, science, commerce, engineering and economics

etc in our society. I will give my view on the causes of the demolition of our

community; it stemmed from the corruption from some of the leaders who are

not educated to deal with social complexities and community development,

but was adamant to lead in order to garner the many benefits of the

programmes implemented by the University of the West Indies. Thus violence

kept escalating and many people continues to lose their lives because the

persons implicated in the wars are not participating in the programmes

because of the leaders who are deemed unfair.

Therefore I am urging all to get involved in a social group which will help

to develop our social skills. The National Youth Service trains and develops

many of our nation's youths for the world of work. I believe that every high

school graduate should get involved in such a venture. The Heart Trust NTA is another excellent programme which caters for the technically equipped individuals. These are just a couple of the organizations which helps youths in Jamaica but there are others worldwide that should be made useful, in order to bridge the gap of employment after secondary school.

These programmes help to develop my social skills and taught me to become multitasked which now caused me to develop a keen attitude to develop my company. The company is called Wowskimusic; it is a company which comprised a record label and clothing line officially registered in 2008. The company was started by two members Garth "Fras" White and Ricardo "Pine" McCalpin. The acronym Wowski stands for wonderful, outstanding, working, strong, kind, individuals.

The name is significant to a movement that is positive, unique and diligent in our quest for greatness. We are true believers in the almighty thus hope to be able to help the less fortunate worldwide. The company is an industry in its bud with a vision of blossoming to benefits of youths from our community, entire nation, entire region and the entire world.

The importance of this story is to highlight the importance of good leadership skills. As the CEO of the company, I had to make certain difficult decisions which would determine the outcome of our company. I had to spend money without caring if I were investing more than my other partners. Many people thought I was stupid to have done that; but as a visionary I could not allow anyone who did not share my views to break my courage and determination to see through our dreams.   Thus good leaders have to possess certain qualities such as:

1. *Strength when others are weak.*
2. *Courage when others are fearful.*
3. *Vision when others are blind.*
4. *Solution when others face difficulties.*
5. *Faith when others lose hope.*

In building our company, it took a lot from us personally, physically, psychologically, spiritually and financially. This is so, as we got involved in the entertainment industry without prior knowledge of how expensive it is to promote a product. Furthermore the market is competitive and the product is affected by a number of negative factors such as payola and bootlegging. I will clarify, these two terms for those who are novice to what is their real meaning. According to the concise Oxford English dictionary, "Payola is bribery in return for the unofficial promotion of a product in the media." However the Broadcasting Commission sanctioned against this type of practice but it is still being done. Even though it is unfair to a financially stricken company like ours, I can understand why it is necessary. It is necessary because the copyright act stipulates that writers, composers and producers of the music being aired should acquire royalties from these large radios and television networks. However our concerns should also be given consideration, because we have to spend a lot of money to get a song to reach market standard. Let's outline the expense of producing a song; for instance a producer has to pay up to J $ 200, 000 to get a good artist on his rhythm. He then has to pay between $ 20,000 and $60,000 to musicians to play the beats. Studio time also has to be taken into consideration and it cost $ 2,000 per hour; then one has to pay $ 5,000 to mix the song. The marketing of the product must now be taken into consideration; thus he now has to think about his promotional tools such as promo cd's, posters and audio-visual materials. The cd's have to meet the criteria of the market standard; therefore it cost to get graphics on proper cd's labels. It also cost a lot to design and print promotional posters. In this modern era it is essential to get a video done for a song; because it can be aired on television and on popular internet sites such as youtube, facebook and myspace. However, this led us to develop creative ways to get our products on the forefront without proper financial support. Bootleg, according to the concise Oxford English is an illegal musical recording. This practice affects every music maker because the consumers are not purchasing cd's; as they can burn them.

Moving away from the technical aspects that affected us; our personal life were also threatened; as our relationships became unstable and even ended. My friends and I, often times laugh at each other when we reflect on the hardships experienced by us trying to build our company. "One of my friends also told me that his personal life between him and his common-law wife is unstable because all his money was spent on building wowskimusic. I told him my relationship between my girlfriend and I have ended; because I was focused on building my company. He laughed but I did not mine." Hungry days, worn out clothes and frustration were a part of our distraught; as many days caught us unable to buy a food to eat while on the road conducting businesses.

We hope to impact the people through our music, fashion, books, social works and create employment for the unemployed in our prospective factories and stores worldwide. We have designed a social programme for boys between the ages 8-18; which will aid in the resocialisation process of youths in our country. If, we reflect on how our society is going then we would see the need for an intervention of the educated people to steer the youths in the right direction. Thus, I am highlighting a method that our company used to help in the empowerment of our boys in my community and I strongly believe in can be done in your community. We have designed a mission statement, state a target, set objectives, designed a philosophy, set activities and evaluate behaviours and performances at the end of the year. I will give an example of our programme design it is called the Wowski and Malaika Foundation:

Mission Statement

We are committed to the holistic development of wellness and healthy lifestyles in our nation's children. Through academics, sports and entertainment; we cater for their emotional, educational, physical, psychological, spiritual, and recreational needs.

Target- Boys between the ages 8-18 in the Hermitage area.

Objectives of the Foundation – at the end of the year we should be able to:

1. Effect positive behaviour changes in each participant of the programme.
2. Help in the resocialisation process of our youth.

Specific Objectives- at the end of the year participants should be able to:

1. Improve on their academic performances at school.
2. Improve on their personal, physical attributes and skills.
3. Improve on their team work and social skills.
4. Improve on moral values and attitude.
5. Improve or develop a positive self esteem.
6. Demonstrate spiritual growth.
7. Develop a level of optimism and courage in approaching tasks.

Philosophy of Programme

We are confident that an early interventionand positive exposure in our young boy's lives will contribute to community and national development. We believe that our boys are at a higher risk of failure in today's society. Thus need more attention and directionality and we can effect positive behaviour changes.

Activities- these activities have to be time tabled or structured; Football, swimming, G-Sat and CXC Subjects, Field Hockey, Games (board, landscape and video) and Parties. I hope this programme design will motivate other people to start something similar to this in their communities worldwide and we would surely effect positive behaviour changes in our youths.

Since coming together from Mona High School; we have been able to establish a duo called "Endocrine". Endocrine is comprised of Pine & Fras; we have been able to complete an album and we are promoting our clothing line. Our other accomplishments are, we and Malaika Entertainment have staged a show called Evolution which was held for two [2] years now. We have now started a mobile massage, exercise program and beauty services; where we provide services for tertiary students and tourists. Also a video was shot for a single from the album called **"Solution"** we have also been able to garner a number of rotation in radio land. Interviews were done by us on radio and television in Barbados, Jamaica and New York; as we are now on the promotional route.

However my passion for music began as early as grade three when I was propelled on the stage by my teacher misses Fenton in her quest to rid me of my shyness. I later understood that she realizes the potential in me but I was afraid to respond to questions even when I knew the answers. I often share this story as I thank my teacher for what she had done to help me overcome my challenge of shyness as I became bold. "She knew about a talent contest at our school but it was for the upper school from 4-6 grades, however she sent me to register for the competition. I was relieved when the organizer told me it was for the upper school and I was in third grade, so I rushed back to my teacher and told her I was not legible to enter. But she got upset and said I should ensure I am involved in the contest, so she went with me to talk with the organizer. I overheard her telling the teacher responsible that she only wanted me to enter to get rid of my shyness; so just let me enter. However the teacher said I could not enter, so deep inside I was delighted but I had to hide it, then she said perform the song and I went and do it as she listened and said I fit the criterion in terms of performing. So I was signed up." This was one contributory factor that caused me to lose my shyness; as I enjoyed the overwhelming response from the crowd. It was important to rid myself of the shyness as it affects ones performance in sports and life skills overall.

These early stages of my life were perfect in shaping my character as the teachers I encountered all played their roles in my development. I must mention that my principal and my coach at Hope Valley Experimental School help in the development of my physical development. It started when I was in grade three, one day I saw the bigger boys kicking football at the goal during lunch break. Therefore I ran and kick one of the balls at the goal and the boy was chasing me to hit me. However the coach called me and said where I learned to kick ball that way and I told him that I watched it on TV. So he told me to attend training the following day; however I did not train because it was intense as I observed it. The next day the captain came to my class and I told him I was attending it later in the day but I did not turn up. The following day

the principal came and commanded me to attend training and I did the

following day. This experience of playing football has built courage and

determination in my character. I have developed a fearless attitude towards

competitive situations and enjoyed challenges. This boldness has help to

develop my self-esteem as many people appreciated my talent. I have

experienced the positive feelings of being a champion; because we have won

the primary league football for three consecutive years and this instilled in me

a passion of winning which followed me through my career. I played for

Elletson Flats Football Club; where I was the most valuable player and leading

goal scorer in the KSAFA Syd Bartlett League. I also represented my college in

the Intercollegiate Competition; where we won 4 consecutive years. I am

interested to see others reaches their paradigm of their horizon and I have

done some work in terms of youth development in my community. I believe

that regardless of how talented or gifted you are; the best thing you will be

recognized for is your humanitarian work. Hence, I am the president of the

Hermitage Emancipation Youth Club and Chairman of the Emancipation Day

Committee; responsible for a youth consciousness seminar on emancipation

day in our community of August Town.

I must give credits to my grade five teacher Mrs. McCalla for believing in my academic potential and she was adamant that I am going to focus on my school work. It remains vivid in my mind when I tried everything to skip private lessons; I told my mother not to pay any money because I wanted to go to training. However my teacher said I should take the lessons regardless of the lack of money; so I still went to training and she came and called me off the field and told me to go into the class. I told my mother that I was not going back to that school because my teacher is pressuring me and she said to me that Mrs. McCalla knew what is best for me. My teacher sat me down and told me that I have tremendous potential and I should focus on my lessons and I told her that I really like playing football. So Mrs. McCalla said that she would allow me to train for one day, so she could watch to see if I had potential in football. She came with me the following day and told the coach to set up a game so she could watch me playing; so he did and I played real impressive. So she said I could go to training but I have to take my lessons from the lunch break; therefore I had to balance my time effectively. Thus it is important for adults to guide our children because it can help to shape the future.

Individuals need to grasp things which are important to their health and well being in the process of, **"Overcoming life's challenges."** Therefore I have established certain secrets which will help people to effectively approach

various challenges in life. However overcoming life's challenges is not solved

on a one time basis; it is a continuous and recurring process. Thus individuals

have to maintain a focus in their quest to tackle the many evolving problems.

I have discovered that many of the challenges we overcame continue to reoccur; one such is sin. Life is filled with tests therefore individuals need to structure their selves in order to overcome the everyday temptations which may cause us to sin. The temptations which we encountered and successful overcame today; may represent itself tomorrow. I must admit it is difficult to go throughout an entire day without committing sins; because I may look at a curvaceous woman and that alone is deem as lusting. However, the problem does not stop there, each day other sexy women continues to appear before our eyes; causing us to lust. Thus individuals have to develop methods which will help us to continue seek forgiveness from the Almighty. The society in which we resides is a main contributory factor that promotes lusting; because where ever I go there are half naked ladies walking around. Thus the government of every country must band certain dress code.

Please see the chapters about **the spiritual realms, professional-academic development and personal development.**

A portrait of Ricardo and Garth in the photo studio

A Trademark Wowski Designz

Understanding Life

There are certain things in this world which are very difficult to understand; especially the controversial word called 'life'. Thus philosophers demonstrate different philosophical views in order to try in explaining our existence. Some express the view that existence precedes essence; which is simply saying we were thrown out on earth without a purpose, while others argue that essence precedes existence; which implies that we were placed here for a purpose, which is to dominate over the Almighty's creation.

There is a dichotomy to every story; therefore individuals can weigh the pros and cons of their experiences to find absolute truth, in order to achieve spiritual actualization and prevent aimless approaches in professing the truth. How can one find the truth? I believe that in finding the truth one should not solely listen to what man says but most importantly what the Almighty says. One should also try to delve beneath the surface and not just view the abstractness of this world, which can just be an illusion. For instance, individuals should not just see creation as it is but query how it came about. I can profess though that there is a supreme being that reigns over all creation.

I am imploring all individuals to find themselves, because for too long now we have lost our identity. "How can one understand life, if we do not first understand ourselves?" There are so many questions that need to be answered, but each individual has to design their own methods of finding answers to certain personal questions, in order to move up the self actualization ladder. Know the person that you are and the needs your life contains. Search deeply to capture the essence of life.

Embedded within life are stages, which I divided into three parts; the base, the body and the apex. At the base one has to initially seek truth, find out what is real. When absolute truth is achieved by an individual it becomes intertwined with their identity and they realized who they really are. By then they develop self esteem, confidence and the greatest virtue, courage. According to a university professor, "Courage is bigger than the battlefield." Hence when an individual knows the truth, and develops an identity, he or she is ready to be associated with a source of happiness. This level of happiness cannot be achieved totally through sexual or financial fulfillment, but through spiritual uplift ment.

Persons may feel a level of peak experiences when all three stages are fulfilled; such persons are self actualized and can be deemed fit in, **"Overcoming Life's Challenges."**

Acquisition of Knowledge

In human beings quest to understand life and ultimately overcoming its challenges; we will eventually have to go on a quest in the acquisition of knowledge. This quest for knowledge was here since existence and will continue until the end of time.

Acquisition of knowledge is very broad thus evolving is a systematic way of imparting and acquiring information called Education, which promulgate branches in organized fields such as science, arts, sociology and business etc.

There is a conflict in beliefs and practices between people in the western world and eastern hemisphere. Westerners believe in a formal education system where individuals study and are rewarded with a certificate to show their qualifications. On the other hand easterners are more comfortable with the broader term 'acquisition of knowledge' where they can seek to acquire absolute truth. This they consider the greatest knowledge of all.

It all goes back to the fact there are two sides to every story; so one needs to examine both sides. This scenario about westerners and easterners was given in order for individuals to evaluate both sides and make an appropriate decision.

I would implore everyone to be willing to seek the absolute truth of the Almighty whilst gaining a good education. I am sure education is important to all as it is the most dominant factor that allows the transition of an individual from a preliterate to a literate state and also provides a nation with the tool to become independent.

Some people may wonder and ask questions such as, "How could anyone not want to seek eternal truth?" and "How could anyone be in disagreement with education?" will continue to arise. But this is one of the most invisible harmful demographic trends; which is so because people in different geographical areas are trapped in different phenomenal fields. A phenomenal field in this case is a specific state of mind determined by culture or religion.

Whether or not we want to believe it, individuals are differentiated by truth or deception. This means there are two set of people in this world one set holding on to eternal truth and the other set holding on to deception whether knowingly or unknowingly. I truly believe in that thus I have created my personal philosophy and I quote, "Though there are infinite differences amongst people of this world the most fundamental difference is one set holding to the eternal truth and others holding on to deception refusing to believe the Almighty is real."

Hence knowledge should be an offspring of the Almighty, this way truthful information can be disseminated from that tree.

Knowledge is the key and many fear that is being used as a destructive tool. It is important that inheritors' knowledge use it for constructive means in the eyes of the Almighty. Those who decide to do the opposite will eventually face eternal punishment.

Once knowledge is adequately acquired and used constructively and truth attained individuals are ready to acknowledge the Almighty.

Acknowledge the Almighty

A race without the knowledge of the Almighty is like a herd of lost sheep. This means they are without a purpose and direction in life. It is important for us to accept that the Almighty is real. This will force us to live a righteous life in the sight of the most high.

His knowledge will cause us to fear his powers, because he is omnipotent, omnipresent, and omniscient. Omnipotence means he is all powerful thus can do anything. This should allow us to respect his powers and be obedient to his teachings. Also this knowledge should instill in us courage in us to fight for what we believe in.

Omnipresence means that the Almighty is everywhere at the same time. Thus individuals should gives all him all the praises because he guides and protects us. Therefore once we pray and ask for protection then it will be granted onto us.

His omniscience means he knows all; since he knows everything we should not live an unrighteous life because his justice is just and fair. "Isn't it wiser to trust the Almighty rather than your initiative?" Human being developing all these knowledge of the Almighty should drive them to do good things in life.

It is also important to know that the Almighty made us in his image and likeness. This means he created us with an expectation to follow his teachings. Once individuals follow his teachings there would be absolutely no violence on earth.

However many of us deviated from his teachings which have resulted in a lot of wars and widespread diseases. Therefore human beings should aim to mirror his teachings and it would resolve many of the problems facing us today. There are a number of holy books scripted with his word; thus we should spend some time researching to find out what is required of us. Once we live by his words then it will lead us to prosperity and eventually gaining eternal life. Holy books are also filled with important information about past, present and future happenings. For instance the meteorological office is filled with dates of past, present and future hurricanes and other natural disasters; therefore whenever they issue their warnings; it is wise to make adequate safety precautions and preparation to go through periods of warnings. Likewise the Almighty issued his warnings so we should make preparation to save ourselves.

These are important guidelines to live by and follow and we will never go astray.

Many unbelievers may ask, "How they cannot see the Almighty?" I would suggest they learn to appreciate the simple things in life such as the air we breathe. Even though we cannot see air; it is very important to life', likewise the Almighty wants us to appreciate him as the creator to whom all praises is due. Human beings need to understand these sign in life.

I always heard my grandmother said that heaven and earth will past away before one of his word past. This means that thine will be done. Thus understanding such things should help us to choose the Almighty as our creator. Individuals should give thanks and praises to the Almighty every time; because he can stop our breath anytime. Instead human beings have been showing little or no regards for the Almighty pursuing their own desires. This is a reason human beings are punished by the most high. Then we complain about the things which are going wrong in our lives and we never seek the Almighty as our saviour.

I am imploring all individuals to follow the commandments of the Almighty. Once these rules are obeyed then all your problems will disappear. Study his word, teachings and follow his path of righteousness and you will be on your way in, "Overcoming Life's Challenges." Another problem many of us faces is that we put the Almighty law at least importance; while we try to follow the doctor's prescription or that of a recipe book. Following your prescription and recipe book may heal a sickness and provides a tasty and healthy meal but failing to obey his commandments will lead to eternal punishment. The western system allows the opportunity for mankind to disobey the Almighty. It promotes a lifestyle which is detrimental to us being tossed into the hellfire. For instance, they use things which suit our desire; such as influencing our food consumption habits sensitizing us to have regular intake. However, the creator recommends a way of life which will guard us against evil; this way of life is fasting. According to Al-baqarah: 2section 23 in the Holy Qur'an, it is stated, "O, believers Fasting are prescribed for you as it was prescribed for those before you, so that you may learn self restraint. Fast the prescribed number of days; except if any of you is ill or on a journey, then fast a similar number of days later. For those who cannot endure it for medical reasons, there is a ransom: the feeding of one poor person for each missed day. Whoever does more good than this voluntarily, it is better for him. However, if you truly understand the rationale of fasting, it is better for you to fast. It is the month of Ramadan in which the Qur'an was revealed, guidance for mankind with clear teachings showing the right way and a criterion of truth and falsehood. Therefore, anyone of you who witnesses that month should fast therein, and whoever is ill or on a journey shall fast a similar number of days later on. Allah intends your well being and does not want to put you to hardship. He wants you to complete the prescribed period so that you should glorify his greatness and render thanks to Him for giving guidance. When my servants question you about me, tell them that I am very close to them. I answer the prayer of every suppliant when he calls me; therefore, they should respond to me and put their trust in me, so that they may be rightly guided. It is made lawful for you to approach your wives during the night of the fast; they are apparel for you and you for them. Allah knows that you were committing dishonesty to your souls. So he has relented towards you and pardoned you. Now, you may approach your wives and seek what Allah has ordained for you. Eat and drink until the white thread of dawn appears to you distinct from the black thread of night, then complete your fast till nightfall. Do not approach your wives during retreat in the mosques during last ten days of Ramadhan. These are the limits set by Allah: do not ever violate them. Thus Allah makes his revelations clear to mankind so that they may guard themselves against evil."

Therefore we need to observe our lives and make the necessary changes to lead to a more spiritual wholesome life. Thus once we acknowledge the Almighty (truth); we are well on our way in, **"Overcoming Life's Challenges."**

Establishing a Purpose

The normal procedure a baby goes through after birth according to Sigmund Freud is anal, oral, Phallic, latency and genital Stages. This scenario is given to demonstrate life as a cycle with various stages of development. Thus in order for individuals to, **"Overcome Life's Challenges,"** they have to make the successful transition from one stage to another. In trying to establish a purpose, this a question we should ask ourselves; why am I here?

Therefore once an individual garner an understanding of life and acknowledges the truth in the Almighty, it means they have found themselves. They are now ready to establish a purpose in life. Due to the fact that many persons are ignorant to the knowledge of the Almighty; they are also unaware of their purpose in life. This lack of knowledge thus led us to our self destruction because of the negative behaviours we often times portrayed.

It is important for us to establish a purpose in life; in our quest to capture life's true essence. This will help to give us direction in life; as it is like a guideline with your goal to achieve success being plotted. Thus individuals can discover whenever they go off track.

Non-existentialist philosophers argued that human beings were thrown out in the world without a purpose. I tend to differ from that ideology because I am sure the Almighty exist and we were made to fulfill a purpose in life. Once we believe that we are here for a purpose then we should fear the Almighty and live by his law.

Imagine they were not a creator governing us then we would not have a responsibility to respect authority or his law. I am sure the Almighty is real because within life is a natural law such as gravity etc. disobeying these law will cause a compulsory effect in the atmosphere and ultimately human beings.

Establishing a purpose will allow individuals to set realistic goals and provide the drive in achieving them. The Almighty greatness is immeasurable thus he instilled different skills in us; thus we should find them and strive towards professional development. This is important information I never knew when I was younger; and apparently neither did my parents understood. Knowledge of this would affect my decision regarding my current career path.

Establishing a purpose is like a guideline to our development; thus once individuals set their goals along the line of their purpose or talents they are well on their way in, **"Overcoming Life's Challenges."**

After individuals have established a purpose in life; they should start to live for a purpose. This will influence us to do what is right in the eyes of the Almighty. Our purpose will shape our character and influence good behaviours. It is important to live by your purpose in order to make a positive contribution to life.

For instance, you have been employed in an organization; you have to live up to your expectation and fulfill criteria on your job description, In order to make a wholesome contribution to the nature of the job.

Maintaining a relationship with the Almighty and evaluation of your life on a continuum is important for us to keep within the scope of our purpose in life. Make necessary adjustments to your actions on a continuous basis to foster improvement in behaviours. Try also to maintain positive impulses which truly reflect your purpose on earth.

Hence individuals, who have established a purpose and are living by it, can consider themselves well on their way in, **"Overcoming Life's Challenges."**

The Almighty's Will Versus Human Desires

In the beginning the creator designed the world and all creations at his will. The most high knows what is best for us. Human beings were created to have dominion over the lesser creatures and serve the Almighty.

However many of us started abusing our powers and being destructive to ourselves and all the creatures; because of our own selfish desires. This is one of the most harmful trends that are plaguing our world today. This is causing an abundance of catastrophe; when human desires oppose the Almighty's will.

Individuals should try and discover what the Almighty will for us rather than desiring the pleasures of this world. Therefore once, you find out what the Almighty will for you; just make them your goals and objectives and try to accomplish them. However once, you are striving for the things the Almighty will for you it is compulsory that it is achieved. "If the Almighty will it to happen, who can stop it?" Anyone who chooses to allow their desires forces them to go against the Almighty cannot gain eternal life.

I am imploring you not to take riches for success because wealth cannot determine your faith in the hereafter.

Let us look at what the Almighty will for us, against human desires. The most high will for us to serve him because there is no other god. However, human desires are the pleasures of this world such as money and material things etc. The Almighty's will for us can only mean blessings and prosperity under his guidance; while human desires are own burden and downfall.

Human desires cause us in most cases to put money above love and material things over human beings. This behaviour is despised by the Almighty and people that possess these tendencies will be punished. The fact that many people value material things over humanity cause it to have very harmful effect on creation, because we were not created with those mal tendencies. Therefore we need to consider the Almighty's will over human desires. Human desires are the main contributory factors to the development of those negative tendencies.

Many people may deny that they possess some of those tendencies, but in truth and fact we would be lying to ourselves. "Do you possess any of those tendencies?" (Yes) or (No). If your response is yes, then you need to pray and ask the almighty to forgive you of your sins. However, if your response is no, then please respond to this scenario. Imaging your mother is on life support and you are required to spend your last savings in the bank to save her; even though the doctors told you that she stand 10% chance of living. Would you give up your last savings regardless? Or would you give the decision to unplug the machine? I am sure many people would not give up their money to save the person.

Going against the Almighty's will cause us to spend more than we can afford. This is so it is like fighting a hopeless battle. Battling the Almighty in reality is senseless because he is the controller of our destiny.

Human desires are what lead to democracy; many of us do not understand the true meaning of such a system. "What is democracy?" according to the concise Oxford English dictionary, it is a form of government in which the people have a voice in the exercise of power, typically through elected representatives. This type of system is very harmful to the lives of human beings because the Almighty have established a will for us to follow. However, democracy created a culture in which human beings can carry out their own desires. This is very destructive to us because people start to perform acts which are undesirable and rebuked by the Almighty. For instance the Almighty stated human beings should have marriage before sex (sacred law), however human beings desires will cause us to have sex with different partners without regards for the Almighty.

Thus I am urging all individuals to allow the Almighty's will over power their human desires. Once this requirement is achieved then you will be well on your way in, **"Overcoming Life's Challenges."**

Communicate with the Almighty

A lot of people regard the Almighty as their father, even though we have never seen the being. However there are empirical evidences to prove that the Almighty is real. We often expect the Almighty to guide and protect our path yet still many of us have not made a relationship with the creator; until facing gross difficulties in our lives.

We need to build a relationship with the Supreme Being; in order to show the much needed appreciation to the life giver, by giving thanks and praises because he is worthy. I will share a story about an elderly woman called winnifred Burrowes who was born on March 16, 1925. She believes strongly in the Almighty; therefore she never forgotten to give thanks and praises. She grew without knowing her mother who died early. Her grandmother took responsibility of her life at 3 years old. She was schooled at Lodge District; where they learned to read and write. It was even more difficult for her as she was a slow learner thus she quit attending school at age 16. Her main belief for overcoming her challenges was humility and calmness which allowed the Almighty to lead her life. She stated everyone should prepare themselves for his return and there is not an in-between truth and deception. This belief in the Almighty was concretised in her heart as she felt the spirit of God flew through her body. This happened one night; as she stole away from her aunt and went to church to listen the preaching of the evangelist, however miss Winnie begun crying. The Holy Spirit hit her to the ground twice and she got up and started speaking in tongues. The spirit had her done seven days of fasting. During that period of fasting the Holy Spirit asked for a glass of water. However, before she could drink the water it had to be consecrated by the evangelist; giving thanks to the Almighty. She had to walk from St. Mary to St.Catherine to buy food at the Market on Fridays; in order to get supply to sell at the Market in Richmond. Obedience is a virtue in one's life; as this is proven by her many journey to and from market. These experiences helped to build in her a level of tolerance to obey the Almighty. This level of Obedience was tested another time. This time the evangelist was preaching and the Holy Spirit overtook her body once again. She went through another seven days of fasting with the intake of only glasses of cold water; which the evangelist prayed over. She was able to overcome her challenges; thus was able to receive that blessing of longevity. She worshipped on the Sabbath day; which is the seventh day of the week. The number seven is symbolic to prosperity and

God's grace. Though she worships on the Sabbath, praying takes place every day. She believes her long life is due to the fact that she honoured her mother and father; so that her days will be long upon this land. She is confident in the Almighty that she even chose the Bible over a gun for protection. She said, "The word of God is sharper than the two headed sword. Man cannot live by bread alone but by the word of God."

"How can someone build a relationship with the Almighty?" individuals need to follow few simple procedures in order to build a genuine relationship with our saviour. We have to first accept the Almighty as the creator of the earth and universe. Then we need to communicate with the most high by praying on a daily basis. Religions may differ on how often people should pray on a daily basis; but I personally thought people should pray as much as possible, just as you would find it fitting to talk with a family or friend.

Prayer is a sacred and universal language that the Almighty cherishes; thus we should make it a family routine. Therefore we need to teach our children the importance of praying. We should begin this practice in the home; just as we taught them how to care for their body, as it will help to develop in them basic ethical values and attitudes. Due to the fact many children are not taught the importance of prayers; we are experiencing a rapid deterioration in moral values in today's society all across the world. Also, because prayers are becoming less than a norm in many homes worldwide and children are not trained to fear the Almighty; they grow with a lack of respect for people in authority. I will give you a scenario, "As a teacher at a prominent high school, I noticed at devotion time we would have problems having the students clasping their hands and closing their eyes to pray. They saw it as disrespectful to them; as they are not obligated to anyone." The essence of the story is to highlight the fact that it is not just that they lack respect for us as teachers, but they felt that they are not obligated to anyone; not even the Almighty.

Prayers are just as important to us as it is for the Almighty our creator of all creations.

1. Prayers signify the acknowledgement and acceptance of the Almighty as the creator.

2. It is basically giving respect to the being in authority over our lives.

3. It is also maintaining a bond with us and the Almighty; because it is essential for us to keep within the scope of the most high.

Thus I am imploring all individuals to take time out of their busy schedules to give praises to the Almighty. There are a lot of distractors such as pornography, video games and computer programmes; that can prevent us from focusing on the saviour. Thus I am urging everyone to continue praying regardless of the devil's gallant effort to lead us away from the Almighty. It is important for us to get personal with the Almighty; because many of us go to church in order for the pastor to pray for us, thinking that is enough glory to the creator. Let us reflect on creation to see the amazing things the Supreme Being have done for us and we would realize the obligations we owe to him. These thoughts should compel everyone to worship the creator every day.

Remembering to pray will cause individuals to maintain a righteous life in the sight of the most high. Once an individual communicates with the Almighty on a regular basis they are well on their way in, **"Overcoming Life's Challenges."**

Many of us cannot identify our greatest challenges in life; because it is sometimes the simple things which we often times overlooked. "Can you identify your greatest challenges in life?" For me, it is the ability to maintain a righteous life in the eyes of the Almighty and overcoming the devil's intentions. Thus, we should try and live within the scope of his requests of us.

Individuals should pray for success in their career goals but most importantly for eternal life. This was emphasized in the book of John 6:27, "So not labour for the food which perishes, but for the food that endures to everlasting life, which the son of man will give you, for the Almighty has set his seal on him."

Therefore in concluding I will reemphasize the importance of prayers in our quest in, **"Overcoming Life's Challenges."**

Spirituality Versus Religion

A lot of people may felt that our world is divided by colour, class and creed but the significant divide is through religion. This is so because each religion practices different ideologies as it relates to worshipping the Almighty. We will not get in depth with the different ideologies being practice by each religion but I will present a logical argument that there are both right and wrong practices in each religion; because people are separated by truth and deception whether knowingly or unknowingly. Thus not everyone who called themselves Christians, Muslims, Hindus or Jews will gain the eternal reward of paradise.

The only way we can end these wars, famines and plaques that are destroying our world; is if religions unite under the Almighty. This is what we need to strive to achieve, and this was mention by Endocrine in one of their song's entitled, "How does it feel?" this is a quotation by Fras, "Religions need to come together like particles in water." Thus, I personally believe for religions to genuinely come together we need to seek spirituality.

Spirituality will allow us to see the Almighty as one and also reflect on ourselves as brothers and sisters without anyone being superior or inferior to each other. Therefore, I must emphasize that all the messengers were sent by the Almighty and they were all sent by the same Supreme Being. This can be justified as they were chosen from amongst us to lead the people in the right way when his message was perverted by the unbelievers. Thus, he sent David with the Psalms, Moses with Torah, Jesus with the Gospel and Muhammad with Qur'an.

Therefore I am urging all individuals to be spiritual in their daily lives. "What do it mean to be spiritual?" according to the concise Oxford English dictionary it simple means, relating to or affecting the human spirit as opposed to material or physical things. Thus the spirit is the non-physical part of the body which is the seat of emotion and character according to the Oxford English dictionary. Hence it is the part of the body which is invisible but is most important to the Almighty and not the garments that are used to cover a lot of our dirty and shameful deeds. It is the part that will leave to face eternal reward or punishment after death.

Therefore I urge individuals to cleanse and make their spirit free so that it can be accepted in the eyes of the Almighty. Human should strive to gain a clean heart and pure mind; this can only be possible once we are truthful to ourselves and the Almighty. We should not allow anyone or anything to prevent us from worshipping the Almighty. It is needless that people attach themselves to a religion and still doing evil works because no one can hide behind their religion on judgement day. Every human being will be judged individually on that day; and no one can cover their deeds with wealth or wonderful garments. Once your spirit is unclean do not consider yourself a part of the Almighty's kingdom. It was written in the book of Corinthians that the person with the least amount of offences will be called into his kingdom first and the persons with the most will be left out; according to their deeds. I personally believes in prophecies and what is said in Corinthians means an insane man; who is dirty by physical appearance may get called into the Almighty's kingdom and some wealthy world leaders; who are clean physically but indulges in evilous deeds, may be casted in the pit of the hell fire.

Therefore I am imploring all individuals who read this book to correct their spiritual life because religions do not save us automatically. Another food for thought is for us to never allow ourselves to be blinded by material things; because the spirit (Character) is the thing which is being judged by the Almighty. I believe that the Almighty uses religion to communicate his teachings to us in human form. However, there is the living spirit in each of us to which the Almighty communicates directly. Hence individuals need to develop a clean spirit which will welcome the creator in their lives. The main reason we have mood swings is due to a relationship between our spirit, the creator and a conflicting demonic spirit. A lot of mornings we woke with a feeling of gloom and sadness, it is the Almighty communicating with our spirit in order for us to cleanse our spiritual lives; which is sometimes confused by the demonic spirit. Therefore it is important to pray regularly in order to cast away evil spirits. This will promote a happy and wholesome lifestyle.

Thus everyone should ensure they overcome this hurdle of maintaining a wholesome spiritual lifestyle. Once this is done individuals are well on their way in, **"Overcoming Life's Challenges."**

<u>Seek Moral Piety</u>

Overcoming life's challenges do not just mean getting over the obstacles in reaching our career goals but also living a righteous life that will gain us eternal life in paradise which is prepared for us. A person may be the richest in the world and still do not have that feeling of fulfillment because he or she lacks the spirituality in their life. Regardless of our academic accolades; moral values is what make us complete, therefore every individual should seek the truth.

Let us examine what is morality; according to the concise Oxford English dictionary it is a system of values and moral principles to the extent which an action is right or wrong. Hence human beings set up their own value own value system to judge whether or not people's behaviour is good or bad. However, it is measured differently at various locations across the world.

Therefore I compel every individual to seek morality handed down by the Almighty because he is just and fair in all situations. Morality is innate in human beings but it is made external by your behaviours. Thus regardless of the difficulties we may face in this world, a good behaviour is still expected of us in the sight of the Almighty. This was stated in John 16:33, "These things I have spoken to you, that in me you may have peace. In the world you will have tribulations; but be of good cheer, I have overcome the world." Do you know what Jesus or any of the prophets have used to overcome the world? It was simply their character, moral principles and truthfulness to the Almighty. Therefore individuals need to be truthful to their selves and to the Almighty in order to overcome this world and ultimately, **"Overcoming Life's Challenges."**

Once a person achieves moral correctness he or she is closer to purity which is important in gaining the eternal reward of paradise.

Looking Through Your Mind's Eyes

The Almighty created human beings with various cells, organs and systems to make up our complete components. However we want to focus on the importance of our eyes. They are very essential for the purpose of sight; they can view animate and inanimate objects but are unable to visualize the invisible components of life such as future happenings.

We should not mistake sight with vision because not everyone with sight has vision nor being blind does not mean one lacks it. Would you think Stevie Wonder lacks vision? He is blind but has managed to establish himself as one of the world most renowned musicians. Stevie Wonder was able to overcome his personal challenges in life; thus I believe everyone can overcome their difficulties with hard work, dedication and perseverance. Therefore individuals should not blame failure on situations but how they approach these situations.

It is important for individuals to start looking through their mind's eyes. This is how all the great men and women visualize their ideas which lead to great inventions, predictions and inspirations. Seeing through the mind's eyes is a treasure for us all. Marcus Garvey looks through his mind's eyes and made some of the most inspirational speeches and also advocates unity and equality amongst human kind. There are other great orators and visionaries such as Martin Luther King and Malcolm X who have look through their mind's eyes and lead and gain the respect from millions of people worldwide.

I am sure the entire world have learnt about the great Jamaican sprinter Usain Bolt; who has accomplished the world records and Olympic championship in both the 100m, 200m and 4x100m events at the 2008 Olympics in Beijing China. This accomplishment was attained through hard work, talent and his ability to execute the instructions given by his coach. However the main reason for completing the triple was his ability to look through his mind's eyes; because an athlete has to run the race a thousand times in their head in order to execute instructions properly on competition day.

- *Bill Gates looks through his mind's eyes and designed computer software; thus he is one of the richest man in the world.*

- *Ben Carson looks through his mind's eyes; thus he has performed one of the most famous neurosurgery in which he separated a cyamese twin who was born with one brain.*

- *Michael Lee Chin looks through his mind's eyes; thus creating success for himself in the insurance business. He is now in the top 100 richest men in the world. He is now able to employ an abundance of people worldwide to work in his various organizations.*

- *Oprah Winfrey looks through her mind's eyes to become a great talk show host and is one of the most powerful women in the world today.*

Many other men and women look through their mind's eyes and have been successful as their visions are able to impact many people lives in a positive way all across the globe. Therefore I am imploring everyone to start looking through their mind's eyes. This can be done by following these instructions:

- Reflective reading- this foster critical thinking in individuals.

- Meditational activities are also recommended to develop thinking skills in individuals.

- Individuals can also seek to develop an enquiry mind that will urge them to seek fresh information by assimilating ideas in the mind's to gain factual data.

- General reading also opens the mind's eyes; therefore we should engage ourselves in a lot of reading and listening activities.

Hence once individuals' starts looking through their mind's eyes, they are well on their way in, **"Overcoming Life's Challenges."**

Developing a Strong Character in the Mind

This topic is straight forward and self-explanatory because individuals should develop a strong character in their minds. This will help to generate internal strength, drive and courage in us to succeed. I will define two terms before moving in to this interesting chapter they are; character and the mind. According to the concise Oxford English dictionary, character is defined as the mental and moral qualities distinctive to an individual. The mind is being defined as the faculty of consciousness, thought and also a person will or determination.

Therefore individuals need to develop a distinctiveness of hard work and dedication to overcome life's challenges. The mind plays a very important role in reaching success in life; because the muscle is just as strong as the mind. In justifying this philosophy I will use empirical evidence to prove a fact. For instance you are in a 100m sprint race at the Olympics Games; in order for you to win that race you have to develop a strong character in the mind, which will provide the drive for you to win the race. If, you do not believe in yourself and ultimately that you can win the race; then your muscles will not permit you to win the race. This is a fact because a race is often times unpredictable because an athlete with the slowest time in the event but have develop a strong character in their mind still stand a good chance of winning.

Let us look at this situation with Jamaica's sprinter Asafa Powell who have performed over 40 sub ten seconds races in his career but has not develop a strong character in his mind; the point is he has not managed to perform well in neither the world championships or two Olympics Games. If, an individual condition his or her mind to believe they are weak; then the muscles will only be able to managed a light work load. Therefore if, an individual is physical weak but set his or her mind to do hard work in order to gain strength then it can be developed by training hard.

The mind is mental- it cannot be described as it is intangible without shape, colour or size, but it can be shaped by our experiences in life. It is something which controls every system in the body and it also helps to influence external factors in one's life such as our vision and drive. Thus everyone should seek to shape their minds with vision, strength and courage in order to overcome life's challenges. Strength in the mind is extremely important in accomplishing our visions; because whenever team members or associates doubts that goals reachable, you need the strength to remain steadfast, diligent and focus when situation of difficulties arise.

Developing a strong character in the mind will allow individuals to concentrate even when there is chaos surrounding us and also help generate focus when it is necessary. Can you imagine being at the world cup, representing your country in the group stages. A penalty kick was awarded to your team and having scored this goal it would qualify your country to the second round? Try to picture the ambience and the atmosphere in the stadium with the amount of cheering all around you. Imagine the amount of people back home that are depending on you to score this goal in order for your country to advance to the next round. The entire spectators in the stadium are nervous but you have to remain calm and focus in order to score the goal. The moral of the story is that individuals have to develop a strong character in the mind in order to, **"Overcome Life's Challenges."** Too many people allow themselves to fail in the mental department; which causes them to fail before attempting specific tasks, so try to prevent that from happening to you. Once you are able to develop a ***strong character in the mind*** you are well on your way in overcoming life's challenges.

Hope versus Faith

Having set your goals and putting action towards achieving them you has venture in to a phase of doubt and uncertainty with a hope of accomplishing regardless. There are two things which help to keep our dreams alive on overcoming certain obstacles in life; they are hope and faith.

Faith is a strong belief or trust according to the Oxford English dictionary, but I saw it as that small reason to continue on my venture. I want to share a stanza from one of my poem about faith,

"Faith is like an ointment, it encourage us through our

disappointments,

It is an anointment, in the darkest times it is

like an enlightment."

This demonstrates an inner belief which causes us to thrive for success even in cases where doubt presents itself. This inner force sometimes helps or is helped by its sister called hope.

Hope is the feeling of wanting something to happen, and thinking that it will happen. It is a person that makes you feel like this according to the Oxford dictionary. It is that external and long term drive which causes us to continue on our quest for success. This creates a drive as you may see someone who has achieved their goal thus emitting in you a sense of optimism (belief).

Individuals should develop a sense of faith and eventually hope and keep them close to us in our quest in overcoming the obstacles in life. Therefore finding your inspiration or talent which is internal is boosted by faith and further encourage by rewards which are external called hope. Believe and trust in the Almighty blessings and you shall, **"Overcome Life's Challenges."**

Perseverance

There is nothing in life which comes easy thus individuals have to be resilient in their quest for success. Perseverance is like output devices on computers, with faith being the central processing unit and hope reflecting storage devices. In explaining this terminology, I mean faith like the c.p.u is internal and dormant but is very important to the entire operation of the human being likewise the c.p.u to the computer. Hope being the storage device means that there is always expectation that work can be produced once it is inputted in the computer. Perseverance is external and active part of the mind; just as output devices on the computer. It is the part that demonstrates how much faith an individual possesses. It is like a printer on the computer; when the information lies dormant in the c.p.u it can still be printed. Just as we believe by faith that the Almighty is real; perseverance is something that gives us the drive to endure the tribulations with the hope of being saved by the Almighty.

Individuals have to learn how to persevere through trying times, let us look at what it means to persevere? According to the concise Oxford English dictionary it is to, "Continue in a course of action in spite of difficulty or with little or no indication of success." Thus, in order to be successful in life individuals have to portray hard work and dedication regardless of the dullest indication of making it. Perseverance is what we need to stay ahead of the game; because life is filled with a lot of competitions. This is essential for us to, **"Overcome Life's Challenges."** Anytime you feel like giving up and to discontinue your quest for success; just continue moving and you will be closer to your goals.

Perseverance is 100% mental strength rather than physical strength. This can be justified in a scenario that will be given, I went to professional development seminar for teachers and the presenter showed us a PowerPoint presentation of Humming Bird. However the moral of the story is to show how much perseverance a bird possesses. The presentation showed the bird's nest being destroyed by different climatic conditions such as snow, storm, earthquake etc. However the bird sings along and work hard a rebuild its nest each time it is destroyed. This story is a real morale booster; as it provides the opportunity for me to look at life differently. It gave me a perspective to work harder without complaining about difficult situations.

Therefore I am suggesting since a bird can go through so many tribulations and still possess that strength to rebuild their nest. Then human beings should just sing along and work hard to achieve their goals and objectives in life.

Our goals and objectives should not just base on career and educational fulfillment. The most important objective we should seek to achieve is that of remaining a believer in the Almighty. This is the time we need to have perseverance in serving the most high; because the Almighty expect his people to endure in his name regardless of the tribulations we have to face in life. It was made clear in the book of Mark, from verse 5-13; but I will quote the final verse, "And you will be hated by all for my name's sake. But he who endures to the end shall be saved." The book also spoke about the wars, famines and beatings the people have to endure. It is stated though, we must not panicked but continue to spread the good news to all the nations in the world. It will take great courage to persevere all these trials that we have to face. Just recites may the Almighty protects us; when you are in difficulties.

Hence, perseverance is the key to, **"Overcoming Life's Challenges."** Once the art of perseverance has been mastered, then we are well on our way in achieving success in life.

Dedication versus making Commitments

It is very important to make a commitment in order to achieve your goals and objectives in life. Just think about this; there are 24hrs in a day, 4 weeks making a month and 12 months making a year. Imagine an athlete not making a commitment to train at the beginning of a world championship or Olympic year; therefore do you think this athlete will be able to give an optimal performance during competition?

Most people who achieve their goals will tell you the amount of hardwork they put in throughout a normal day. I am not a prophet but if an individual is uncommitted to something it will affect the longevity of it.

Commitment is like a promise which enforced dedication in an individual and vice versa. Marcus Garvey was dedicated to his commitment of empowering black people, thus he travelled all over the world to spread the message of unity amongst his people. He even died in exile carrying out what he set out to do.

I am therefore imploring all individuals to make a commitment and dedicate themselves to achieving their goals and objectives. It is not easy reaching them but whenever you feel like stopping press on.

 Make a commitment to serve the almighty and try very hard not to break it and you will be well on your way in overcoming life's challenges.

 Make a commitment to be faithful to your relationship and stay dedicated to not breaking it.

 Make a commitment to achieving your goals, thus take some time out of each day and dedicate yourself to put in some hard work. In order to effectively carry out the work; one can think about the rewards that will be achieved by making the commitment.

Hence once an individual remain steadfast to his or her commitment and dedication they will be well on their way in, **"Overcoming Life's Challenges."**

Decision Making

Most successful people today are so because of sound decision making skills applied in ambiguous situations. Don't make reckless decisions and expect the almighty to work a miracle for you; a decisive thinking skill is required to achieve success. Individuals will have to make decision in order to propel themselves to higher levels in life. One incorrect decision can cause failure in your life which can cause a down fall for a lifetime.

Therefore individuals have to first identify the problem on goals for which a decision needs to be made. Then identify all the possible solutions. The next step is to measure the advantages and disadvantages of each items proposed. Then select the most appropriate item; which may be beneficial to your development.

Everyday people have to make decisions, thus it is important for us to begin to make sound decision from an early age. Even though individuals have to make their own decision in life; it is better to have the input of others it is called advice, by the way, 'what is an advice?'According to the concise Oxford English Dictionary it is, guidance or recommendations offered with regard to future actions. ***** Individuals should now be able to weigh the pros and

cons of the input being given and make a firm decision.

GET INVOLVED IN SOME SORT OF PHYSICAL ACTIVITY

It is important for individuals to take part in some of physical activities which promotes a healthy and wholesome lifestyle. There are many ways in which people can develop a fit and healthy lifestyle; either by involving in sports, exercising and even gardening. However the involvement in sports will enhance an individual's cognitive, affective and psychomotor development. The cognitive has to do with the mind, which is the practical knowledge of a sport. It also enhances your thinking skills. The affective domain is also influenced, as it allows for better co-operation and team work which is required in schools and corporate organizations. Individuals can learn through sports to appreciate and respect others. With psychomotor development taking place individuals will learn to put theory into practice, which is essential in the educational field and working world today.

Physical activities also promote physical, emotional, psychological, spiritual, educational and social wellness for humans. Physical wellness means that individuals can develop their fitness, muscular enhancement and the whole physical well being of individuals."What is fitness?" According to the concise English dictionary, "it is having the requisite qualities or skills to do something competently."Therefore I think every individual should try to gain a level of physical fitness to carry out their daily chores. Thus when an individual is fit, it is the better the circulation of blood around the body. Therefore when physical wellness is achieved, the body would be better able to carry out strenuous work. Emotional wellness is also achieved through physical activities because individuals can join groups to carry out various activities. This will give them a sense of purpose and acceptance by others. Often time's people tend to live a monotonous lifestyle, meaning they just go from home to work and return home, which is not healthy to their physical, social and emotional well being, because it lacks physical and social activities. Physical and social activities will alleviate the emotional disturbance in individuals. This will help them to live a happier and more sociable life which will enhance their emotional status and promote better interaction between them and others, either at school, or work. Once emotional wellness is achieved individuals are well on their way in overcoming life's challenges.

The psychological needs are also catered for physical activities. This is enhanced as daily goals are achieved, thus instilling in individuals courage in taking on challenges and also confidence and positive spirit towards overcoming obstacles in life. This kind of attitude is what is required by your teachers at school or employers at work. Sometimes there will be challenging tasks that needs to be accomplished but being equipped with the psychological well being, even the unreachable will seem reachable. Once psychological wellness is achieved, you are well on your way in overcoming life's challenges.

Spiritual wellness is also achieved through physical activities as the more competitive individuals become in sports, is their higher the appreciation for the Almighty. For instance, the higher the competitiveness of the individual, the more it will require for them to pray, asking the Almighty for victory over their opponents. I am sure most teams who are involved in competitions are taught by their coaches to acknowledge the Almighty before a game or race. The spiritual well being is most important in the eyes of the Almighty. It was deeply emphasized in a chapter of this book called "Spirituality versus Religion." Therefore once spirituality is achieved; you are well on your way in "overcoming life's challenges.

A lot of people may feel that they are too occupied with their jobs and school assignments to even get involved in physical activities, but sports cater for the educational wellness in human beings. For example, individuals are educated about tactics, strategies and execution of different skills, in order to defeat their opponents. These things can also be applied in the working world in order to stay ahead of the opposing company in your field. This also promotes time management which is important for personal development, which will affect you for a lifetime. I can testify for this. Listen to this scenario. I was in fifth form in high school and preparing for my exam and I was the only from my class who was playing Manning Cup Football for my school, all my friends were telling me to stop playing because they thought I would not get enough studying time. But I was able to manage training and studying hard at the same time. Hence this could not prevent me from passing my exams. Therefore once you achieve educational wellness, you are well on your way in "overcoming life's challenges".

Social wellness is also achieved when individuals get involved in physical activities, whether recreational or competitive sports, this generates in individuals, greater respect and appreciation for others, due to the fact that they are associated with a group. It helps in bringing vibrancy to their life and helps to promote a wholesome and healthy lifestyle in them. This also helps us to function better in our school groups and professional life which requires energy to get work done adequately. Once social wellness is achieved, individuals are well on their way in "overcoming life's challenges."

Therefore I implore all to get involve in some sort of physical activities, as it helps to lower the risk of health related diseases such as hypertension, coronary heart diseases, diabetes and obesity. I am sure once individuals are spiritually, psychologically, educationally and physically healthy, they are well on their way in, **"Overcoming life's challenges."**

STRENGTH VERSUS WEAKNESS

Strength is our belief in God and confidence about our gifts and talents, while weakness is the characteristics in humans that alter development. On the quest for success, individuals need to learn how to deal with situations such as good and bad, win and lose, likewise their strengths and weaknesses. Everyone is created with strengths and weaknesses, thus each person must identify them. Since life is a test, we should always aim to overcome obstacles in order to pass it. After identifying and classifying them, we now have to look at the positive side of both. Thus we should spend a lot of time working on our strengths and also our weaknesses. Life is filled with challenges; hence individuals have to identify the strengths within the realms of life. Our strength lies within our belief in the Almighty, because He is our strength. So do not be fooled for a minute that He is weak. The devil will always try to tempt us with wonderful material things to lure us away from God. My brethrens, these things are of no real value; being saved in the end of this life is what really matters. God urges His people to develop *strength of virtue and character* thus individuals should try to develop such in order to maintain a good reputation in the eyes of the Almighty. Strength in character will prevent us from getting weak and blaspheming against God in times of famine, plague and troubles. This is so because if the distinctive moral qualities are developed in us, then even in hard times, strength in character will cause us to repent of our sins and glorify His name. This is expected by the Almighty.

Establish strength in faith; also when the journey to your goals in life gets tedious and looks unpromising, remember that it is strength in faith that will allow us to endure tribulations and be saved by the Almighty. I am encouraging all individuals to hold on to their faith in the Almighty and never let anyone prevent you from believing in Him. A lost in faith is destruction to the entire being. *Develop strength in mind and body*; this is essential because our mind determines what we can or cannot do. Therefore once we believe that it can be done, and then we can achieve it. Thus we have to mold our minds to be strong, and a lot of obstacles in life can be overcome. A strong mind will allow us to be proactive and productive in our thinking. It eliminates fear from us and turns impossibilities into possibilities. "How can we mold our mind?"I believe individuals have to set challenges that are realistic. First start from the easiest obstacle and then upgrade the challenges gradually, by overcoming them each, step by step. We do this by practicing to be positive that we can overcome any obstacles that we encounter.

Once your strength has been established and developed, you now have to work on correcting your weaknesses. It is important to correct your weaknesses because they affect our performances. It was stated that "a chain is strong as its weakest link" Therefore we must work on sealing up the weak links in our chain. For instance, look at this scenario of Asafa Powell, former world record holder, a Jamaican athlete. He could be considered the world's fastest man, but whenever he is at grand track and field meets, he always fails to perform at his best. This is so because he is not accustomed to the many rounds in a championship. I am sure Powell's coach will be focusing now on his weakness of not being able to sustain the rounds and try to get him managing the rounds at his next championship. Individuals should not settle for less when they can do better. In certain situations, they are only failure or success, heaven or hell, there is no in between. If your weakness is going to prevent you from entering heaven, then you should work on that weakness. Sometimes our weaknesses override our strength and determine an untriumphant outcome of many talented persons, but we need to establish and develop our strengths so that they can override the weaknesses in order to, **"Overcome life's challenges."**

Winning Versus Losing

These two terms are both character builders; thus individuals need to understand that life inculcates winning and losing. Human development is depends on how they approach these situations over time. Winning seems to instill in us optimism, high self esteem, courage, self confidence and appreciation for others. On the other hand losing seems to generate fear, pessimism and low self esteem in us.

In examining the characteristics of winning and losing, a couple of questions do arise. They are, "Who is a winner?" and "Who is a loser?" secondly "Are they natural winners versus natural losers?" According to the Oxford dictionary, a winner is something or someone very successful. However, my personal view is that it is someone who accomplishes their aims and goals and is able to maintain a stable relationship with the Almighty. According to the oxford dictionary a loser is someone who loses a game. Personally, I believe that when someone loses a game they are not deemed a loser but when refuse to try harder and giving up in the process; refraining from their attempt in becoming successful, that is the time you can consider them losers. Let us look at Usain Bolt he ran in the Olympics in 2004 in Athens Greece and was beaten.

He went home and train harder and came back in the Beijing Olympics in 2008; where he won three gold medals and break the world records in all events in which he competed. I am imploring you all to rise to the occasion and never give up in your quest in reaching success in life.

In addressing the question are they natural winners versus natural losers? It can be considered vary, it all depends on each individual finding their own talent. The multiple intelligence theory demonstrates that individuals possesses and even states that every individual inherits more than one.

Therefore once an individual accept the contrast of winning and losing and is determine to find methods to develop themselves personally; they are well on their way in, **"Overcoming life's challenges."** For instance a person who loses often can work harder to prove critics incorrect about their perceptions of a born loser. Hence once that obstacle is crossed it proves that even the most desolate can overcome life's challenges.

<u>Love Versus Hatred</u>

There are two sides to a story; likewise a coin has two sides. Love and hate are opposite of each other but they work hand in hand. Love is a natural force embedded in us, which can either strengthens to become stronger or weaken to become hate according to our experiences at an early age. For instance a child who was nurtured by him or her parents would normally grow with a sense of trust or love. Another child that was ill-treated or neglected by him or her parents tends to grow with a level of mistrust or hate.

It is important for every individual to incorporate love in their life; in order to fulfill the Almighty's request of us. "Do you think life's challenges ends on earth? I do not think so; I believe it will determine whether individuals gain eternal rewards or punishment. It should be admitted that for us to show love is really challenging because it is very difficult to forgive and forget someone who is destructive to you. However, we should remember that the Almighty has forgiven us on many occasions; thus, regardless of what happens to us we should let love determine our decisions.

Hate is the opposite of love; it is destructive, it is not regarded by the Almighty. We should try our best to disseminate these thoughts from our minds in our quest in, **"Overcoming life's challenges."** Malicious thoughts are self destructive; it only forces individuals to live a contradictory life departing from the Almighty's request of us. The Almighty commands us to live in love; therefore we should do our endeavour best to fulfill his request. Love is stronger than hate thus more people appreciates it; and the few who makes hate a stronger component of themselves are allowing life's challenges to overcome them. I can prove that more people in this world appreciate and associate themselves with love than hate. I want everyone who read this book to answer this question, "Would you prefer to have a government who is insane with the Almighty's inner beauty or a rich man doing evil duties? This question is a real moral tester, I wish I could get your responses but I am sure there are more believers than non-believers in this world.

I am sure that people with love in their heart gain more heavenly praises than those with hatred onto mankind. Therefore I am imploring all individuals to make love become a part of their life in order to, **"Overcome life's challenges."**

Humility Versus Aggression

It is important to examine your personality to discover if there is distinction in your life between humility and aggression. Even though individuals should establish a balance between both; on a wider scale humility should outweigh the latter. This is essential as it allows us to reflect on life circumstances; thus permitting self control. Individuals need to allow themselves space to think constantly because failing to do so can cause us to entangled in all sort of trouble.

However aggression plays its part in certain situations such as in sports. For instance it is the nature of certain games which requires aggression in order to foster success. This is when one's aggressiveness should be displayed; however it needs to be controlled by your humility. My grandmother usually told me that, "humble calves sucks the most milk." I did not understood what she meant but later on in life, I realized that she meant once you are humble more people will appreciate and would probably help you through your problems. You will also learn a lot more through being calm and focus rather than loud and boisterous. This is so because a patient person can learn from the mistakes impatient persons made.

I once read a sign on the wall of a probation office, it stated; "Patience is the greatest power." It reinforced what I have experienced back then in second form in high school. It was a rainy day and class had ended, I was sheltering on the school corridor along with other students. I begun to lose my patience after an hour and half had passed and it was pouring even heavier, so I decided to leave in the pouring rain. I was soaked from head to toes. Then after 5 minutes the rain stopped. Since I was walking home my friends ran and catch up with me. So when we reached about quarter mile from home we realized that it had not rained in our community. However I was still wet so everyone was asking why I was so wet? I told them that I was walking and it was raining at my school. They thought I was ridiculing them as my friends were dry as ever. However, the moral of this story is that individuals should demonstrate a level of patience and this come with humility.

Once an individual captures the essence of being humble and let humility precedes aggression they are well on their way in, **"Overcoming life's challenges."** In proving this I will leave you a food of thought. A teenage herder boy went to hunt a bull to provide his family with dinner. The bull was wild and furious and the boy's approach. The herder had a bush knife and the bull was so aggressive he began attacking the young herder. The boy quickly took off his shirt and began teasing the bull with it, this cause the bull to focus on the shirt as his target. Therefore he attacked the target a number of times until he became tired, he was stabbed in the throat with the knife. The humble herder began to cut the cattle to provide his family with food. It was stated by the Almighty that individuals should be, "Humble and they shall be exalted." Hence once you have exalted yourselves then you shall be humbled. Humility teaches human beings to satistify; as this is a detriment to our desires. International reggae superstar Sizzla, spoke about this in one of his popular song. The line stated, "A bird in the hand is worth more than two in the bushes." Aggression and greed can cause you to lose yourselves through not satisfying. It is ultimate to grasp a sense of humility in, **"Overcoming life's challenges."**

SURPASS MISTAKES

"The man without sin cast the first stone."This biblical scripture can be interpreted in a sense that no one is perfect thus we are all prone to mistakes. Let us look into what is a mistake. According to the concise Oxford English dictionary, "it is something that is not correct or an inaccuracy."Even though human beings are prone to mistakes, we should try our endeavored best to avoid making them. Many people may wonder to themselves "how can they avoid making mistakes?" Most of them can be avoided if individuals think thoroughly about what is the most appropriate option before taking an action in doing something. "Prevention is better than cure," I always hear my grandmother using that statement and reflecting on it, it is a fact. Thus individuals should try and learn from the mistakes of others, since most of the mistakes that we have and will encounter in life, have been made by others. So prevent yourself from making the same ones. Another way to avoid making mistakes is to ask questions and get professional advice in certain situations. It is important to get expert analysis in order to prevent making mistake in life. For instance, individuals need to seek medical advice from a doctor when faced with a medical problem. Do not assume the position of your illness but consult a doctor to diagnose the problem. Making a mistake can cause the condition to get worse.

Individuals should also read and do research to get an in depth knowledge about something before delving into it. A lot of people would like to be successful in life but doesn't possess the knowledge that will see through their visions. For instance, David would like to invest his money into a business. He does lots of reading and researching to understand the nature of the business and other important things which are important to the business being successful. After garnering full knowledge and he is satisfied with what the result will be, he went ahead and started his business. The way David approach his new business plan is the correct way and he stands a good chance of not making much mistakes. Since we have examined what are mistakes and how we can avoid making them, we must transfer our knowledge into action. My football coach always emphasized to our team before each game that "the team that makes the least mistakes will be the winner. Reflecting on this statement I saw where it was factual. This is so because if one team failed to outplay the other team and end up losing the game, it means that they have made one or more mistakes than the other. Therefore we should try our best to make no or the least mistakes as possible.

In following this topic of "surpassing mistakes" many people may start to develop a fear of making mistakes, Individuals should release the fear of making mistakes from their mind. Fear paralyses the actions of human beings, thus on your journey to succeed, don't worry about making mistakes but how you will surpass them. Even if you failed on your attempt of being successful, don't give up, just assess the situation and make the necessary corrections. Thus individuals have to be open to corrections and changes. Do not live in denial of your mistakes but be able to accept them and make the corrections, also pray and ask the Almighty to cleanse you of your sins and guide you along life's pathway. It is very important to consult God before making any major decision in our lives, as this will lessen the chances of us making mistakes. Many of us have made numerous mistakes in our life, thus we should ask for forgiveness, make the necessary corrections and go on. Therefore once individuals can surpass mistakes, they are well on their way in **"Overcoming life's challenges."**

PERSONAL DEVELOPMENT

Human beings can only complete when they are able to master these three aspects of life; the spiritual realms, academic professional development and personal development. We should always strive to develop ourselves as a person. Although we are unique in our own ways, there are certain behaviours that we should try to instill in us. Some of these traits includes: discipline, moral values, ethics, good etiquette, attitude and hygiene. Some of these traits are hereditary but all of them can be adopted. In order for an individual to be successful in overcoming life's challenges, they have to develop a level of self-discipline. Let us examine what is discipline? According to the concise Oxford English dictionary, "it is the practice of training people to obey rules or a code of behaviour." Therefore discipline will help us to live within the scope of the laws and prevent us from getting into trouble. It will also help individuals to be diligent in their jobs. It also helps us to follow instructions, thus not falling into the wrong track. I am imploring all individuals to exercise discipline in their quest for success in life. My grandmother always says "manners will carry you throughout the world.' This statement is so true because having discipline will allow people to appreciate us. It will also make it conducive for people to work with us. One should always remain ;**{1}-Disciplined to the teachings of God. {2}- Discipline towards career goals. {3}-Discipline towards your school work and your jobs. {4}-Discipline towards your morality. {5}-Discipline towards your established purposed.** Once you are able to establish and maintain a disciplined character, you are well on your way in, **"Overcoming life's challenges."**

Now let us look at values. One should know their values in order to make a positive contribution to humanity. Therefore as individuals, we should all set a standard of behaviour which is socially acceptable by everyone regardless of demography, class or creed. We should value humanity over money or material things. This will enable us to develop ethics, which is important in corruption prevention in today's world. Thus everyone should value: **{1}-Self {2}-Others {3}-God.**

When I was in college, my vice principal always used a statement that emphasizes the importance of developing a good attitude towards work. He always said "your attitude determines your altitude." This means that our attitude will determine how far we reach in life. Therefore everyone should develop a positive attitude to work hard, in order to effectively overcome life's challenges. It is also important to develop a positive attitude as it helps others to judge your character or personality and also fosters cohesion between students at school and staffs at work. Individuals should develop positive attitude towards :{1}-God {2}-their career goals {3}-people {families, friends, the poor}. {4}-community -development. A positive attitude towards the Almighty will give us a great reward of eternal life. However our humanitarian work is what we will be recognized for most. Once you develop a positive attitude, you are well on your in **"overcoming life's challenges."**

Ethics is also important in these aspects of life: {1}-spiritual development {2}-professionalism {3}-personal development. Let us first examine the word ethics. According to the concise Oxford English dictionary, "it is the moral principles governing or influences conduct." So it is basically a guideline between right or wrong. Ethics can be measured differently in different societies. However we should strive to measure it based on what is right in the sight of God. A person that develops ethics will save themselves from: corruption, falsity and fraud, bribe, eternal punishment and deception.

Therefore I am imploring all to establish good ethics in their life, in order to overcome life's challenges.

Hygiene is also important to our personal development and is essential in your professional and spiritual development. We have to learn how to care for our bodies, as it relates to our cleanliness and health. A proper hygiene is important to our self-esteem. Hence we make sure that we always bathe properly, brush our teeth regularly, use deodorants and other perfume agents and comb our hair. This will give us the self-confidence needed to approach daily tasks and people. Thus everyone should strive to establish a proper hygiene. In concluding, I am urging everyone to develop themselves personally, in order to, **"Overcome life's challenges."**

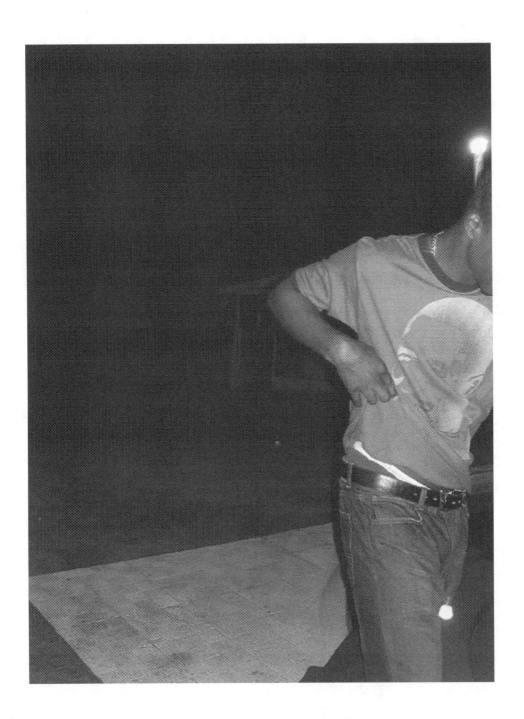

A Picture of Wowski Designz

EVALUATE YOUR LIFE

In any profession, evaluation is essential in measuring performance, however it is also for life's process on a whole. Educators in their quest for success, uses different assessment tools to measure student's progress. Likewise in the medical field, doctors have to evaluate the effectiveness of drug treatments to cure diseases. Therefore it is important for us to evaluate the progress in our life on a continuous basis. First and foremost, we should identify the thing that needs evaluation. Individuals should evaluate their life on a three prong approach, these are: spiritual, professional and academic progress and personal development. In evaluating your spiritual life, you need to focus on certain essential things, such as, acknowledging and communicating with the Almighty, moral piety, understanding life, acquisition of knowledge, spirituality versus religion and establishing a purpose. Evaluate yourself to find out if you have really acknowledged the Almighty. Ensure to live a practical life based on His teachings. A problem that is being overlooked by many is a lack of communication between us and God. Therefore individuals should check themselves to see how often they pray, if any at all. A lot of people allow themselves to be preoccupied by work or fun activities, thus not enabling them any time to pray. I am imploring all to remember to pray without ceasing, and all our problems will be solved, also our spiritual life will be enhanced. Moral piety is very essential in our quest for righteousness in the sight of the Almighty. Evaluate to see how morally pious you are, in order to make necessary corrections in your life. Therefore every individual should seek moral piety which will aid in ethical decisions and good portrayal of behaviors. Once an individual is morally pious, the less exposed they are to sinful deeds and the closer they will be in overcoming life's challenges. Once individuals evaluate themselves to find out their understanding of life, they will develop a better approach in dealing with life. Then you should evaluate yourself to find out how much knowledge you have acquired. Hence the more knowledge you have acquired, the better able you are in overcoming life's challenges. Individuals should also check to ensure that they are fulfilling their purpose in life. Thus you should reflect on your actions and make necessary adjustments which will enhance our livelihood. Evaluate yourself to see if your emphasis is on spirituality with God or religion. Try your best to ensure that your goal is to gain spiritual righteousness rather than dominance in religion. I admit that religion plays an important role in gathering people to worship God. However it also causes people to differ on certain ideologies, causing segregation amongst people around the world. If your emphasis is on spirituality, then we would come to the acceptance that there is only one God, and we must all come together as people and worship Him in the beauty of holiness in one fashion and one accord. Therefore we must focus on our spiritual life with God and not on the different religions. Once your spiritual life has been evaluated, you are well on your in **"overcoming life's challenges."**

Evaluation in our academic and professional life is also very important for further development. For us to effectively upgrade our lives, we should look at a number of themes including controlling our mind. Academically or professionally, individuals need to take control of their mind in order to overcome life's challenges. So evaluate to see if you are someone who has looked through your mind's eye. It is important to look through your mind's eye in order to accomplish great things in life. Evaluate also to ensure that you have developed a strong character in the mind. Check to see whether you are easy giving up or if you are fearful in attempting tasks which seems impossible. If you have any of these signs, then read the chapter on 'developing a strong character in the mind." Evaluate your actions to check if there is a balance between hope and faith in your life. In order to test hope and faith, you need to assess how you approach difficult situations. A person with great hope and faith always approach difficult situations with great optimism. Evaluate your life to check the current level of perseverance you possess. It is important for us to develop a high level of perseverance as we go through our education, career and life because it is what keeps us pressing on even when our goals seems unreachable. Without perseverance, we will never be able to overcome life's challenges. Evaluate to see how dedicated and committed you are in reaching your goals in life. In being dedicated and committed, you have to set your priorities straight and be willing to make sacrifices for them. There is no success without sacrifice. If you are successful without having to sacrifice, it means that someone has sacrificed before you. If you sacrificed without success, it means that someone will be successful after you. So once you are dedicated, committed and willing to make sacrifices in reaching your goals, you are well on your   way in **"overcoming life's challenges."**

Evaluate your decision making skills in order to help with your professional development. Once your decision making skills are direct and developed, then you should use it effectively to solve the problems that you will encounter in life. Evaluate to see if you are physically healthy. Physical activities are very important to our longevity, thus it is important to discover how physically fit we are, as it rids us of many chronic diseases and makes us better able to give our best professional or academic performance. Evaluate your lives to see how you deal with situations such as strengths and weaknesses. Ensure that you develop and enhance your strengths and work on your weaknesses. Evaluate to find out how you deal with winning and losing. Always aim to win and work harder when you lose. Evaluate to find out how humble or how aggressive you are. It is being humble in some situations and being aggressive in other situations that cause you to fail or succeed in life. Always ensure that you use humility and arrogance in the appropriate situations at all times. Evaluate your life to ensure that your love has outweighed your hatred. Many of us lacks love, therefore we need to garner a lot of love in order for us to avoid doing evil deeds towards each other.

Evaluate your life to ensure that your personal development is on par with renowned persons that are successful in life. Ensure that you are also on par with your checkmarks such as discipline, moral values, ethics, attitude and hygiene. Test yourself to ensure you have demonstrated a high level of self discipline towards the Almighty, education and your career goals. Once you have attained a result, make the necessary adjustments which will foster further development.

Once all these aspects of your life have been evaluated, then you can make the necessary adjustments and be well on your way in, **"Overcoming life's challenges."**

A Brainstormer- writes down one of your challenges in life and use a three prong (spiritual, academical-professional development and personal development) approach in overcoming that challenge. Individuals can mail their response to www.myspace.com/wowskie

A Portrait of Wowskimusic CEO's

Printed in the United States
by Baker & Taylor Publisher Services